COMPUTER PROGRAMMING FOR KIDS

An Easy Step-by-Step Guide For Young Programmers To Learn Coding Skills (2022 Crash Course for Newbies)

Dexter Rogers

1

TABLE OF CONTENTS

INTRODUCTION

Welcome to the world of computer programming for kids, or the act of writing a program to tell your computer what to do what should I do? A series of commands are used to write programs instructions in a specific language, three of which I am fluent in will be discussing – Java, SQL, and C++.

Computer programming is not as difficult as it appears, and it can be learned As long as you do it correctly, it can be a lot of fun. I've put together a basic

"Good day, World!" Just to give you an idea, there is a tutorial for each of the three languages. You'll get a sense of how everything works. Aside from that, I've also included some helpful hints for newcomers and common blunders. When it comes to programming, novices tend to make mistakes. Simply put, a programming environment is a piece of software that allows you to create programs.

On the system, write, compile, and run computer programs. It is correct a connection between the programmer and the computer Convert the programs you'll be writing into the computer's language and instruct it to do the same for you. As a result, before you pick up any programming language, make certain to inquire about the prerequisites programming environment and how to set it up. You intend to use a computer for your programming course.

It is necessary to delve deeper into the programming environment and its configuration consisting of three basic components, namely a text editor, a compiler, and an interpreter. You will almost certainly require all three of these elements for your course So, before you start looking for them,

Let us explain what they are and why you will benefit from them. They are required.

Text Editor

A text editor is a basic text tool that allows you to create text files in which you will write your code. The extension of the text file will vary depending on the programming language you are using; for example, if you are programming in C, your text files will have the extension. If you are working on a Windows system, just type Notepad into the search box and use it as a text editor for your applications. You may also look at Notepad++ for more advanced settings. It is freely accessible, and all you have to do is download and install it on your system. If you are a Mac user, you may look at text editors like BBEdit and TextEdit.

Compiler

Now that you've created the program and are ready to check whether you did it right, you must run it through the computer to see if it understands what you're trying to say. The computer, on the other hand, only understands binary language, and what you've typed is far from what it can immediately consume. As a result, this file must be converted to binary format.

If you committed syntactical mistakes or did not follow the rules of the programming language, the compiler will not be able to complete the conversion smoothly and will display an error message to you.

As a result, a compiler is a software that checks to see whether you followed the syntactical rules of the programming language in question and transforms the text file to binary form. Furthermore, this conversion procedure is known as compilation.

Most programming languages, including C, Java, C++, and Pascal, among many others, need compilation, and you must install their corresponding compilers before running any programs created in them.

Interpreter

Other programming languages, such as Python and Perl, do not need a compiler, in contrast to the ones described above. As a result, rather than a compiler, they need an interpreter, which is also software. The interpreter simply reads the program from the text file and, as it parses the file, converts and executes the contents. If you're working with any of these programming languages, be sure you have the appropriate interpreter installed on your machine before you begin.

If you have never dealt with a computer before or have little to no expertise installing software on a computer, you should get technical assistance from an expert. However, be sure to conduct the installation manually since it will help you get acquainted with the equipment you will be working on within the near future.
+
Furthermore, if your computer does not allow the installation of any of the programming environment parts, you may utilize the online compilers and interpreters that are now accessible for all programming languages. You just need a decent Internet connection and a web browser to access these online resources and begin your programming classes and practice sessions right immediately.

WHAT IS A PROGRAMMING LANGUAGE AND WHAT ARE THE MOST POPULAR PROGRAMMING LANGUAGES?

Computer programming languages are classified into three types:

Programming Language for Machines:

This is the standard computer language, which includes rudimentary commands that are conveyed to the computer in binary code. As a result, if you wish to teach a computer, you must use binary code. Here's an example of a binary 'hello world':

Language of the Assembly:

Machine languages are replaced by assembly languages. Mnemonics are used to represent machine language commands. Because computers cannot comprehend assembly language, we employ an assembler to translate assembly language code into machine language code. Assembly languages are simpler to learn and use than machine languages, but they are nonetheless laborious since they are closer to machine language.

High-Level Programming Languages:

The late 1990s ushered in the development of a new generation of computer programming languages called high-level programming languages.

High-level programming languages are English-like computer programming languages that are platform-agnostic, which implies that code written in a high-level programming language may execute on any system or computer.

Almost every programming language in use today is of the high-level kind. Statements are used in these languages to command a computer to execute groups of instructions. Here's an example of a current programming language being used to calculate the sum of two numbers:

    Number1 = 10
    Number2 = 100
    Sum = Number1 + Number2

We now have a plethora of high-level programming languages. The list below contains the most prominent programming languages, which are frequently used in any area.

- Python
- Java
- C++
- JavaScript
- Ruby

In this course, we will go through the fundamentals of programming or creating computer code in three programming languages: Java, C++, and Python (version 3).

The next portion of the discussion begins by looking at the fundamental aspects, comprehension of which will help you to get started on the road to becoming a good programmer.

Programming Fundamentals "

High-level computer languages, like human languages, contain a set of important components. The main parts of most high-level programming languages are as follows:

- Environments
- Keywords
- Data Types
- Variables
- Operators
- Control Flow
- Functions
- Arrays
- Strings
- Inputs/Outputs

Configuration of the Environment

Because computers cannot directly comprehend high-level programming languages, we employ a translator or converter to create our code and then translate it to machine code. This is referred to as a development environment.

Setting up your development environment, although not a programming aspect in and of itself, is frequently the very first step in working with any programming language. It consists mostly of installing a certain sort of software on your computer for you to produce computer code and convert this code into a language that your computer can comprehend.

The most noteworthy tools required to construct a traditional programming environment with most high-level programming languages are:

9

Text Editor

A text editor is a piece of software that allows us to write computer code in plain text without any styling. Notepad is the default text editor in Microsoft Windows. The term "source code" refers to the code created and saved by a text editor.

Translators

Translators are used to transforming source code into binary code. The binary code is then converted into what programmers refer to as 'object code.' Translators may work as:

1. Assemblers are used to translate low-level languages into machine code.

2. Compilers: Compilers translate source code to binary code, which is subsequently executed. If the program encounters an error during execution, the compilation process terminates without producing a binary. C, C++, Objective-C, Swift, and Pascal are the most popular compiled languages.

3. Interpreters: Interpreters are similar to compilers in that they transform the code line by line rather than executing the complete program. This implies that each line of code is executed until an error occurs. When a program produces an error, the interpreter pauses and communicates the error.

Python, Ruby, JavaScript, and Perl are the most popular interpreted languages.

4. Hybrid Translators: Hybrid translators combine compilers and interpreters. They translate the source code to Bytecode. The bytecode is subsequently translated and executed by runtime engines. The Java Virtual Machine is the primary example here (JVM).

NOTE: Configure your programming environment by the varied instructions provided by each of the three programming languages we will be working with—each language has its own set of environment setup instructions.

11

PROGRAM EXECUTION AND PROCLAMATION

What Exactly Are Statements?

Before I explain what, a statement is, allow me to ask you a simple question. When was the last time you had to select between two options based on factors such as what you want, what you can afford, what is nearby, and what is not? When we make choices, we take into consideration several factors and variables that will ultimately affect our conclusion. Similarly, to assist us with such situations, we employ statements, which is precisely what we shall investigate.

Statements are just instructions that the program interpreter understands and executes; we have been creating some ourselves when we assign values to variables.

Assignment statements are statements in which we assign values to variables. However, as long as the Program is being addressed, statements normally relate to 'if' statements.

The 'if' statement is what presents a scenario to Programs and enables Programs to take appropriate action 'if' a certain circumstance is true; otherwise, it follows a different path. It seems to be simple, yet it is also intriguing. Let's explore how to write our first 'if' statement.

Here's what's going on. A person would want to sign in using their account.

The popup merely asks for the passcode. If the user enters the correct, case-sensitive passcode, he should be able to get access. If a user enters the erroneous password, it should not proceed to notify the user that the password supplied was incorrect.

To do so, we must first create a password. You may either construct your own pre-defined one or request that the user establish a new passcode and then re-enter it. I'll leave the decision to you.

```
password = input ("Create a password: ")
print ("Welcome to the portal")
```

So far, I've just requested that the user input a password of their choosing. You may use any text or number as a password if you choose. I then made a little welcoming greeting. Now we'll ask the user for their password:

```
password_check = input ("Please enter your password: ")
```

The only difference here is that I modified the variable's name. If you're wondering why, it's because if I had used the same variable name, the password would have been changed rather than compared. We'll need to use a separate variable if we want to validate the password.

The consumer has now provided us with two pieces of information. If the password matches, we instruct Programming what to do.

```
if password_check == password:
print ("Successful! Welcome back!")
```

There are two things to keep in mind here. When you put 'if' as your first word, PyCharm recognizes that you want to build an 'if' statement. The color of 'if' will change to reflect this. We must specify our condition after 'if.' You may have noticed that I used "==" instead of a single equals symbol to accomplish this. These indicators are known as Operators, and we will go over them in more detail later. Here's everything you need to know:

'=' is used to assign a value

'==' is used to either equate two variables or compare to see if the two are exactly the same.

This comparison operator will be used in the preceding example. The most intriguing part is that, unlike all of the other programs we've written so far, this line finishes with a colon ':'.

In Program, every conditional statement, such as the 'if' statement, is followed by a colon to establish a block of code that will run after that colon. An indentation will be used to start the following line. Remove that indent since it would create confusion because I had previously established the condition, which says "If password check is precisely the same as password," and now I added the command that must be executed if the condition is fulfilled. When you run this software, you will get a screen requesting you to enter a password. This is saved as a variable called password. The message will then ask us to key in our password again for verification or login reasons. Whatever we write here will be saved in the variable password check. Programs will now compare the two numbers to check whether they are identical. If this is the case, it will print a success message.

I am certain that you purposefully attempted to input the incorrect password. Isn't it true that the program was abruptly terminated without any warning? There's a good explanation behind this. Only the 'if' condition has been specified. We never got around to defining the 'otherwise' condition.

The last condition is the 'otherwise' condition, which normally comes into action when the 'if' condition or others are not true and are not met.

To do this, we will add two lines of code underneath the first. The full program should now look something like this:

```
password = input ("Create a password: ")

print ("Welcome to the portal")

password_check = input ("Please enter your password: ")

if password_check == password:

print ("Successful! Welcome back!")


else:
print ("Sorry buddy! That's a Nay!")
```

Notice how the 'otherwise' sentence requires no indentation and does not need you to specify any more criteria.

Now I'm going to execute the code twice. Let us examine how it works once one is accurate and the other is incorrect:

Correct password

Create a password: 123

Welcome to the portal

Please enter your password: 123

Successful! Welcome back!

Incorrect password

Create a password: 123

Welcome to the portal

Please enter your password: 122

Sorry buddy! That's a Nay!

15

Here's a thought: what if a statement has more than one condition? How would we go about choosing a number between one and three and then sending an appropriate message based on the number the user selects?

```python
print("Welcome to my little game")

number = int (input("Choose a number between 1-3: "))

if number == 1:

print("You love to consider yourself a leader, don't you?")

elif number == 2:

print("You hate being alone, right?")

elif number == 3:

print("The more, the merrier, is it?")


else:

print("Really? You can't follow simple instructions, can you?")
```

It's a very common method of putting things, but the only thing to notice here is the 'elif' statement. The 'elif' is sandwiched between 'if' and 'else,' where 'it' is the first condition and 'else' is when none of the requirements are fulfilled.

Yes, I am aware! It should have been called 'ifel,' but it is what it is!

Try it out for yourself by checking each of these with different numbers as your options. Use any number larger than three for a little fun and see what happens.

This is how Conditional Statements are handled in Programs. If you're a player, you've probably encountered games where your choices may affect the end of the game. You've identified the perpetrator!

There is no limit to the amount of 'elif' statements that may be used. You may make as many as you want. With that stated, let's spice things up a bit.

Conditional ('if') statements that are nested

Assume we use the same numbers as before, but this time we want to include an 'if' statement inside an 'if' statement. Assume we want our user to pick another numeric value, this time in decimal numbers, but only if the user chooses the initial value as the number.
Examine the code below and attempt to figure out how it will be performed.


```python
print("Welcome to my little game")

number = int(input("Choose a number between 1-3: "))

if number == 1:

print("You love to consider yourself a leader, don't you?")

number2 = float(input("Enter a number with a decimal figure between 1 and 2: " ))

if number2 == 2.00:

print ("Okay! I meant a little lesser than that!") elif number < 1.50: print("Oh, come on! You can go higher!") else: print("You know what, forget it!")

elif number == 2:
```

print("You hate being alone, right?")

elif number == 3:

print("The more, the merrier, is it?")

else:

print("Really? You can't follow simple instructions, can you?")

Within the first condition, we added another variable. If the user chooses one, the popup will ask the user to input another number. Because the entering number will be a decimal figure, we utilized the conversion here to convert it to afloat.

We then added another condition that determines the upper and lower limits. To make things a bit more interesting, there is no right number to select from here. Regardless of whatever option the user selects, they will either get a notice stating that they got a bit too high, or one encouraging them to go higher. The remainder will always be perplexing to the user.

A Nested Statement is a conditional statement inside a conditional statement. If the user chooses a number other than the triggering point, this whole block of code may be skipped.

Execution

Iteration in programming refers to the repeating of lines of code. It's a necessary quality in computer programming that aids in problem-solving. The primary pillars of algorithm development are iteration and conditional execution.

Let us begin with the:

Whereas Statement

How would you tackle the challenge of writing software that can count to 10,000? Will you sit down and write 10,000 printing bills? Although you can, it will take a significant amount of time. Computers, on the other hand, often count; in fact, computers may count incredible quantities. So, there must be an escape route. You must print the value of a variable and then continue the operation until you reach 10,000. Looping is the process of repeatedly running the same code. While and for are two unique statements in program language that manage iteration.

FUNCTIONS, INPUT, OUTPUT

Functions

During this phase, you will learn how to easily create functions in a program. Functions are a set of codes that are meant to do a certain purpose. If you want to develop a program that will do a certain job, you must specify the function and call it. In addition, I will show you how to feed information to functions and display it on the screen.

Sometimes the easiest way to explain something is to provide an example.

The following program is a welcome program that prints a message.

```
def welcome_user():

" " " Transmit a Welcome Message."""

Print ("Welcome to Learning Programming.")
welcome_user()
```

This example demonstrates the most basic framework of how a function works. The first line tells the interpreter that you wish to create a function by using the keyword "def." As a result, anytime you see the term "def" and the word that follows it, it denotes a function definition. The parenthesis fulfills its duty of containing the necessary information. After the parenthesis, the function definition is followed by a colon.

When you see an indented line after declaring a function, it is the function's body. The second line is known as a docstring, even though it is a remark that defines the function's purpose.

Docstrings are typically surrounded by three quotations. The third line also includes the message "Welcome to Learning Programming."

This line includes the function's primary message. This indicates that the welcome user's principal task is to print "Welcome to Learning Programming."

If you wish to call a function, you must first put the function name, followed by parentheses and a colon. Our program's output will look like this:

Welcome to Learning Programming.

How to Pass Data to a Function

We'll change our example to show how to give information to a function. We may modify the software such that it not only says "Welcome to Learning Programming," but also includes the user's name. To do so, we must ask the user to provide their name.

```
def welcome user(name):

    """"Transmit a Welcome Message."""

    Print ("Welcome to Learning Programming, {name.title()}!")

welcome user("Thomas")
```

When we input welcome user ("Thomas"), the function welcomes user() is called and the name "Thomas" is sent to the

21

function to perform the print command. Our products will be as follows:

Welcome to Learning Programming, Thomas!

Arguments and variables

We created a function that asks the user to provide a value for the variable username. You immediately call the function and provide it a value; the message is printed in the print() method. A variable is contained inside our function. In Program, the variable is an example of a parameter, while Thomas is an argument.

Arguments are information-containing values that are sent from a function call to the function. For example, when we called the function, we sent a value into it. In this case, the parameter is "Thomas," and we gave the data to the function.

NOTE: Both names are used interchangeably. As a result, when you see a function definition referred to as an argument or vice-versa.

How to Pass an Argument in Program?

Because a function definition may have multiple parameters, a function call can similarly have multiple arguments. It implies that you may give your argument to a function in a variety of ways. You have the option of using keyword arguments or positional parameters. The argument in the latter must be in the same order as your parameter, but the argument in the former consists of a variable name and its corresponding value.

22

Positional Arguments

Because each argument in the function must correspond with a parameter in the function defining section, this is the easiest method to send an argument in Program. Let us develop software that displays animal information to see how this works. In this case, the function informs us of the kind of animal and the pet's name.

```python
def animal_list(animal_kind, pet_name):

""" Display Details About Animal."""

print(f "\nThis is a {animal_kind}.")

print (f "My {animal_kind}'s name is {pet_name.title()}.")

animal_list ("Cat," "Lucy")
```

The first piece of code inline specifies a function. It denotes that the function needs the kind and pet name of a specific animal. We gave the animal type and pet name after creating the function. In the function call (animal list), for example, we assign Cat as the animal type and Lucy as the pet's name. Our output will provide information on the animal Cat with the pet name Lucy.

```
This is a Cat.
My Cat's name is Lucy.
```

Using Several Functions

We are free to call the function as many times as we want. All we have to do now is add another argument to our function. Look at the code below:

```
def animal_list(animal_kind, pet_name):
 """ Display Details About Animal."""

print(f "\nThis is a {animal_kind}.")

print (f "My {animal_kind}'s name is {pet_name.title()}.")

animal_list ("Cat", "Lucy")

animal_list ("Dog," "Bruce")

animal_list ("Rat," "Chase")
```

The program executes the same sequence and produces the same result.

In this case, though, we added two additional criteria to the list.

As a result, our output will look like this:

```
This is a Cat.

My Cat's name is Lucy.

This is a Dog.

My Dog's name is Bruce.

This is a Rat.

My Rat's name is Chase.
```

24

When you have several arguments, calling a function numerous times is an efficient technique. The code for the animal's information is written just once within the method. However, if you wish to describe a new animal, all you have to do is invoke the function by supplying information about the animal.

Arguments for Keywords

This is a name/value pair sent to a function. Inside the argument, you must explicitly connect the value and the variable name.

There will be no misunderstanding when you send the parameter to the function this way. Let's change our prior code to call our animal list utilizing keyword parameters ()

```
def animal_list(animal_kind, pet_name):

 """ Display Details About Animal."""

print(f "\nThis is a {animal_kind}.")

print (f "My {animal_kind}'s name is {pet_name.title()}.")

animal_list (animal_kind ="Cat", pet_name= "Lucy")

animal_list (pet_name= "Chase", animal_kind ="Rat")
```

Our first four lines have remained unchanged. There is, however, a distinction between the final two sentences. When the interpreter sees the fourth line, it invokes the function and sets the parameters Cat to animal kind and Lucy to pet name. Because the order doesn't matter when working with keyword arguments, the following line will execute the same action. As a result, the last two lines of code are equal and deliver the same result. Our above-mentioned program will show:

This is a Cat.

My Cat's name is Lucy.

This is a Rat.

My Rat's name is Chase.

To prevent errors while utilizing keyword arguments, verify that the correct parameter names are used in the function specification.

Default Setting

In addition to the keyword parameter and position argument, each parameter in a function might have a default value. If you supply a parameter that is provided in the function, the value is used by the program.

If no parameter value is specified, Program uses a default value for the parameter.

```
def animal_list(pet_name, animal_kind = "Cat"):

""" Display Details About Animal."""

print(f "\nThis is a {animal_kind}.")

print (f "My {animal_kind}'s name is {pet_name.title()}.")
```

---

animal_list (pet_name= "Lucy")

Compare this code to the previous one. Did you notice anything interesting in the first and final lines? The animal list function, on the other hand, is used to define a specific animal type, using Cat as the default value.

I have a Cat.

My name is Lucy.

It is important to note that the parameter order inside the function declaration must be modified since the default value makes specifying the specific animal species as an input meaningless. As a result, the sole parameter accessible in the function is the pet's name.

Basic Interactivity Functions

In this phase, we will identify the two most significant functions for interactivity in Program, which are print() and standard output, respectively. The standard input, on the other hand, is input(), as we shall explain below.

Standard Output

The print() method is used to show information through the standard output, which is generally the computer screen.

In Program2, print is a reserved word, however in Program3, print() is a function, thus the content must be written as a parameter inside a function, or, to put it another way, it must be enclosed in parentheses.

27

```
interactivity.py  ×

1      print("Output")
2      print("The end")
3
```

As we can see in this basic example, we use print, and two strings, "Output" and "The end," should display on the console.

It is crucial to note that there are many circumstances when you have two strings variables, and it is occasionally required to utilize both in the same print; hence, we continue to concatenate and print the two strings of characters together.

Standard Input

The default function for Program3 is input(), which is responsible for retrieving some input value given by the user; it must be allocated to a variable so that you receive a string. An important feature of this function is that you can also display a message on the screen, allowing you to show users what they need to enter and that the programmer can write a message that tells what type of data has to be entered, for example, to tell the user that they need to enter a natural number to calculate the area of a rectangle, but to understand this a little better, consider the following example:

```
interactivity.py  ×

1      var1=input("Put a number:")
2
```

In this example, we can see that the variable that was initialized, var1, is equal to the entry that the user enters, which should be a number because the function instructs the user to enter a number. However, the same entry will become a string because the function input() always returns a string, and from there, you can perform the calculations.

Escape characters: These are character combinations that behave differently within strings because they allow us to do things we couldn't do otherwise, such as insert a line break.

\\	\
\'	'
\"	"
\a	Sound
\b	ASCII regression
\f	Page advance
\n	Line break
\r	Carry Return
\t	Horizontal Tabulation
\v	Vertical Tabulation
\ooo	Octal value character
\xhh	Hexadecimal value character

Triple quotes: are used to put multiline character strings. They may be used with single triple quotes '''text''' or triple double quotes """text""". Here's an example of how it might be used:

```python
1  string='''Hi
2  how are
3  you
4  '''
5  string2= """This
6  is
7  a
8  example"""
9  print(string+string2)
```

In this example, we generated two variables, string, and string2, and utilized both triple single quotes and triple-double quotes to insert numerous line breaks without the requirement for escape characters, in this instance without the n. Finally, we will output the concatenation of the variable string and string2 on the screen.

WEB PROGRAMMING

This section describes web programming in a nutshell. The Internet is become a fundamental thing for many individuals. Pr's explanation of web modularity

HTTP (Hypertext Transfer Protocol)

Communication is an amazing thing. It enables information to be transferred between people. The chemical element and mating signals are sent out by the animals. People say lovely things to their partners to convey their affection. The hunters whistled as they silently gathered their prey. The server ordered two orders of fried chicken and beer from the kitchen. The Pharaoh's pyramids endure the curse of barred access, while traffic lights control traffic and television advertising disseminate. Everyone is linked to the world around them because of communication. Individuals participating in the mysterious process of communication usually follow a precise routine. We employ standard grammar in our regular conversations. When two individuals employ distinct grammars, they communicate using various protocols, and, ultimately, they don't understand what they're saying.

The flow of information between computers is referred to as computer communication. As a result, computer communication should adhere to the Communication Protocol Conference as well. A multi-level protocol system is used in computer communication to accomplish multi-level worldwide Internet communication. The most used sort of network protocol is HTTP Protocol. The Hypertext Transfer Protocol is its full name.

The HTTP protocol allows for the movement of data, particularly hypertext files.

It is the most frequently used Internet Protocol in the modern era. In reality, when we visit a Web site, we often put an HTTP URL into the browser, such as http://www.google.com, which indicates that you must utilize the HTTP protocol to reach your site.

HTTP functions similarly to a fast-food order:

1. **Request:** A diner requests a chicken burger from the server.

2. **Response:** The server answers the customer's request based on the scenario.

Depending on the circumstances, the waiter may answer in a variety of ways, including:

- The Drumstick Burger is prepared by the waiter and served to the diner. (Everything is OK.)

- The waiter was assigned to the dessert station.
He sent his clients to the proper counter to place their orders. (Redirects)

- The server informed the diner that the Drumstick hamburger was no longer available. (Cannot be located)

When the transaction is completed, the waiter places it behind him and prepares to serve the next client.

GET /start.html HTTP/3.0

Host: www.mywebsite.com

There are three messages in the first line:

- Get the method. Describe the action you wish the server to carry out.

- /start. The location of the HTML resource. These are links to the server's index. The HTML files.

- HTTP version 3.0. HTTP 3.0 was the first commonly used version, while the latest version is 3.3.

The GET method was the only one available in the early HTTP protocol. The server receives the GET request and sends the requested resource to the client via the HTTP protocol. This is analogous to ordering and receiving a Burger from a client. The POST method is the most often used technique in addition to the GET method. It's used to send data from the client to the server, with the data to send attached to the request. The data sent by the POST method is processed by the server. A header message is included in the example request. The host is a sort of header information that gives the address of the server you wish to reach.

Following receipt of the request, the server will create a response, such as:

HTTP/3.0 200 OK

Content-type: text/plain

Content-length: 10

Jesus Christ

Three messages are included in the first line of the response:

- HTTP 3.0: Protocol version
- 200: Status Code
- Ok: Status Description

OK is a textual description of the status code 200 that is only for human consumption. The computer is solely interested in three-digit status codes. The status code is 200 in this case. Everything is OK, and the resource returns properly. The class to which the server answered is represented by the status code.

There are several additional popular status codes, for example:

- 302, Redirect: I don't have the resources you're searching for here, but I know someone who does. It can be found there.
- 404 Not Found: I'm unable to locate the materials you're searching for.

The next line, Content-type, specifies the kind of resource included in the body. Depending on the type, the client may launch various handlers (for example, displaying picture files, playing sound files, and so on). The length of the body portion in bytes is indicated by content length.

The remainder is the reply's body, which comprises the primary text data.

The client obtains the requested resource from the server through an HTTP transaction, which is the text in this case. The above is a high-level description of how the HTTP protocol works, with many intricacies omitted. We can then examine how the Program interacts with HTTP.

Package http.client

HTTP requests may be made using the client package. As we've seen, the host address, request method, and resource path are all critical pieces of information for HTTP requests. Simply explain this information, as well as HTTP. You may make an HTTP request using the client package.

The Python code is as follows:

```
import http. Client
connection                                                          =
http.client.HTTPConnection("www.facebook.com")
    #hostaddress conn.request("POST", "/") # requestmethod and
resource path

    response = connection.getresponse() # Gets a response

    print(response.status, response.reason)# Replies with status
code and description

    content = response.read()
```

Object-Oriented Programming (OOP)

We'll now look at the four object-oriented programming ideas and how they relate to Python.

Inheritance

The first significant notion is referred to as "inheritance." This refers to the ability of one object to derive from another. Take, for example, sports automobiles. Vehicles are all sports cars, but not all vehicles are sports cars. Furthermore, all sedans are vehicles, but not all vehicles are sedans, and sedans are most definitely not sports cars, even though they are both vehicles.

This Object-Oriented programming principle states that objects can and should be split up into as few and precise notions as feasible.

This is accomplished in Python via deriving classes.

Assume we have a new class named SportsCar.

Vehicle(object) class:

def__init__(self, makeAndModel, prodYear, airConditioning):

    self.makeAndModel = makeAndModel

    self.prodYear = prodYear

    self.airConditioning = airConditioning

    self.doors = 4

```python
def honk(self):
    print "%s says: Honk! Honk!" % self.makeAndModel
```

Now, construct a new class named SportsCar, but instead of deriving from the object, we'll derivate from Vehicle.

```python
SportsCar class (Vehicle)
    def__init__(self, makeAndModel, prodYear, airConditioning):

        self.makeAndModel = makeAndModel

        self.prodYear = prodYear

        self.airConditioning = airConditioning

        self.doors = 4
```

We don't need the honk function here; just the constructor function is required. Declare a sporty car now. I'm going to stick with the Ferrari.

```python
ferrari = SportsCar("Ferrari Laferrari", 2016, True)
```
Now test this by calling

```python
ferrari.honk()
```

After that, save and run. Everything should go off without a hitch.

Why is this the case? This is due to the concept of inheritance, which states that a child class inherits functions and class variables from a parent class.

It's a simple enough notion to comprehend. The following one is a bit more difficult.

Polymorphism

The concept of polymorphism is that the same process may be carried out in several ways depending on the circumstances. In Python, this may be accomplished in two ways: method overloading and method overriding.

Overloading a method means defining the same function twice with different parameters. For example, we might provide our Vehicle class with two distinct initializer procedures. It currently assumes a car has four doors. If we wanted to specify the number of doors on a vehicle, we could add a new initializer function below our present one with a door's parameter, as seen below (the newer one is at the bottom):

```python
def __init__(self, makeAndModel, prodYear, airConditioning):
    self.makeAndModel = makeAndModel

    self.prodYear = prodYear

    self.airConditioning = airConditioning

    self.doors = 4
def __init__(self, makeAndModel, prodYear, airConditioning, doors):

    self.makeAndModel = makeAndModel

    self.prodYear = prodYear

    self.airConditioning = airConditioning

    self.doors = doors
```

Someone may now choose whether or not to declare the number of doors when making an instance of the Vehicle class. If they do not, it is believed that the number of doors is four.

Method overriding occurs when a child class uses its code to override a parent class's method.

As an example, create a new class named Moped that extends Vehicle. Set the doors to zero, which is ludicrous, and the air conditioning to fake. The only arguments that matters are the make/model and the year of manufacture. This is how it should look:

```python
class Moped(Vehicle):
def__init__(self, makeAndModel, prodYear):

    self.makeAndModel = makeAndModel

    self.prodYear = prodYear

    self.airConditioning = False

    self.doors = 0
```

It would now honk if we created an instance of the Moped class and executed the honk() function. However, it is well known that mopeds do not honk, but rather beep. So we'll replace the parent class's honk function with our own. This is quite easy. In the child class, we simply redefine the function:

```python
def honk(self):

print "%s says: Beep! Beep!" % self.makeAndModel
```

I'm one of the 299,000,000 Americans who couldn't identify a make and model of Moped if their lives depended on it, but you can test it out for yourself by declaring an instance of the Moped class and testing it out.

Abstraction

Abstraction is the next key topic in object-oriented programming. This is the idea that the programmer and user should be kept away from the computer's inner workings. This offers two advantages.

The first is that it reduces the inherent security concerns and the danger of catastrophic system malfunctions, whether caused by humans or not. By isolating the programmer from the inner workings of the computer, such as memory and the CPU, and sometimes even the operating system, there is a minimal possibility of a misstep resulting in irrevocable harm.

The second benefit of abstraction is that it naturally makes the language simpler to grasp, read, and learn. Though it reduces the language's strength by removing part of the user's control over the complete computer architecture, this is exchanged for the ability to write fast and effectively in the language, without spending time dealing with trivialities like memory addresses or the like.

These are applicable in Python because, well, it's quite easy. You can't go into the computer's nitty-gritty, or do much with memory allocation, or even precisely allot an array size, but this is a tradeoff for excellent readability, a highly safe language in a very secure environment, and simplicity of use with programming. Compare the following C code snippet:

```
#include <stdio.h>

int main(void) {
```

```c
printf("hello world");

return 0;

}
```

to the Python code for doing the same thing:

```python
print "hi, world"

#That's all. That's the only thing there is to it.
```

Abstraction is typically a net advantage for a vast majority of programs produced today, which is why Python and other object-oriented programming languages are so popular.

Encapsulation

Encapsulation is the last important notion in object-oriented programming. This is the simplest to explain. This is the idea that common data should be grouped and programming should be modular. I'm not going to go into detail since it's a really basic idea. Classes are as simple an illustration of encapsulation as you can get: common characteristics and methods are bound together under one coherent structure, making it very easy to make objects of the like without having to generate a ton of hyper-specific variables for every instance.

So there you have it. We had finally concluded our Python trip. First and foremost, I'd want to thank you for reading through Python for Beginners: The Ultimate Guide to Python Programming. Let us hope it was instructive and provided you with all of the tools you need to reach your objectives, whatever they may be.

The next step is to put this information to use. You just made one of the finest choices of your life by learning the foundations of Python, whether as a hobby or a career move, and your objective now should be finding ways to utilize it in your day-to-day life to make life simpler or to do tasks you've wanted to complete for a long time.

DEEP LEARNING AND MACHINE LEARNING COMPARISON

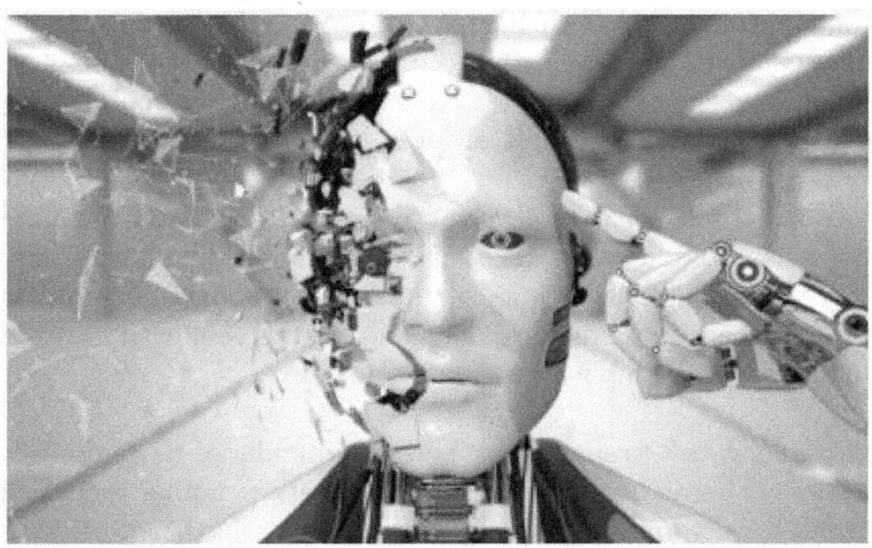

Artificial intelligence is a topic that has come up in several discussions throughout the years. This was a future notion that was popularized in movies and comic books a few years ago. We are presently enjoying the pinnacle of artificial intelligence after years of development and study. Indeed, it is generally predicted that AI will help usher in a new era of computing.

Artificial intelligence Machine Learning and Deep Learning may have some similarities, but they are not the same thing. Many individuals use these phrases interchangeably without thinking about the consequences of their assumptions. Deep Learning and Machine Learning are artificial intelligence knowledge fields. While numerous definitions have been used to describe artificial intelligence in the past, the general standard is that this is a process in which computer programs are constructed with the ability to operate and function as a normal human brain would.

The goal of AI is to teach a computer to think and operate in the same manner that the human brain does. When it comes to the human brain, we have yet to completely comprehend its true potential. Experts think that even the most bright people on the planet are unable to completely use their brain capability.

As a result, since we have yet to completely grasp and test the boundaries of our brains, how can we construct computer systems that can imitate the human brain? What if computers learn to communicate and function like humans to the point that they can fully use their brainpower before we do?

Ideally, the strength of AI and the boundaries of its thinking ability are yet to be determined. Researchers and other specialists in the subject, on the other hand, have made significant progress throughout the years. Sophia is one of the most recent instances of AI that upholds these ideals. Sophia is now the most sophisticated AI model in the world.

Given our failure to fully push the boundaries of our brains, we may never fully push the limits of AI to the point where they can totally replace humans.

Machine Learning and Deep Learning are two disciplines of artificial intelligence that have seen a lot of study and development in recent years. The focus on these frameworks stems mostly from the fact that many of the world's major technology businesses have effortlessly adopted them in their products and integrated them into human life. On a daily basis, you engage with these models.

Machine Learning and Deep Learning have certain characteristics; however, they are not the same. Similarly, when comparing these two to artificial intelligence. As a novice, it is important to understand the distinctions between these programs so that you can seek out and discover wonderful possibilities to develop your abilities in the business. There are now numerous employment vacancies in Machine Learning and Deep Learning in a world that is constantly spiraling towards more machine reliance. In the near future, there will be even more as individuals hurry to adapt and incorporate these technologies into their everyday operations and lifestyles.

Machine Learning vs. Deep Learning

Before we begin, it is critical that you review the fundamental definitions or explanations of these two topics. Machine Learning is a subfield of artificial intelligence that teaches computers how to learn via algorithms. Aside from methods, Machine Learning models need input and output data from which they may learn via interaction with various people.

When developing such models, it is usually a good idea to create a scalable project that can accept fresh data and utilize it to maintain training the model and increase its efficiency. An effective Machine Learning model should be able to self-modify without needing your input while still producing accurate results. It learns from structured data and constantly updates itself.

Deep Learning is a subset of Machine Learning that employs the same algorithms and functions as other subsets. Deep Learning, on the other hand, goes beyond the power of algorithms by introducing layered computing. Deep Learning algorithms are utilized in layers, with each layer processing input in a different manner. Artificial Neural Networks are the algorithm networks utilized in Deep Learning.

The term Artificial Neural Networks refers to the most recent version of what occurs in Deep Learning frameworks. The idea here is to attempt to emulate how the human brain operates by concentrating on neural networks. Deep Learning Sciences experts have examined and referenced several studies on the human brain throughout the years, which has aided in the advancement of research in this subject.

Approaches to Problem Solving

Consider the following scenario to better understand the distinction between Deep Learning and Machine Learning.

Assume you have a database with images of vehicles and bicycles. How can Machine Learning and Deep Learning be used to make sense of this data? At first sight, you will see a collection of vehicles and bicycles. What if you need to differentiate photographs of bicycles from photos of trucks using these two frameworks?

To assist your Machine Learning algorithm in identifying photographs of trucks and bicycles based on the categories specified, you must first train it about these photos. How does the Machine Learning algorithm distinguish between the two? They do, after all, have a striking resemblance.

A structured data method is used to find the answer. To begin, identify the photographs of bicycles and trucks in a way that identifies various aspects that are unique to each of these products. This is enough information for your Machine Learning system to learn from. As it meets additional data, it will continue to learn and develop its knowledge of the difference between trucks and bicycles based on the input labels. It will continue to look through millions of additional data points to identify the difference between trucks and bicycles just on this single image.

How Do We Address This Issue in Deep Learning?

The method used in Deep Learning differs from that used in Machine Learning. The advantage here is that with Deep Learning, you don't need any labeled or structured data to assist the model to distinguish between trucks and bicycles.

The visual data will be identified by the artificial neural networks through the network's many algorithm layers. Each layer will recognize and characterize a distinct characteristic in the photographs. This is the same strategy that our minds use while attempting to solve an issue.

In general, the brain evaluates a large number of alternatives before deciding on the proper one. To identify a solution, Deep Learning Models will route queries via numerous hierarchical processes. Deep neural networks identify certain identifiers that aid in differentiating bicycles from trucks at each identification level.

This is the most basic method to comprehend how these two systems interact. Deep Learning and Machine Learning, on the other hand, may not be suitable approaches for distinguishing these images. As you learn about the distinctions between these two domains, keep in mind that you must first describe the issue properly before deciding on the best technique to take in order to solve it. Later in your adventure into Machine Learning, which has been covered in the advanced volumes in this series, you will discover how to pick the proper strategy.

We can see from the above example that Machine Learning Algorithms need organized input to distinguish between trucks and bicycles. After finding the classifiers, they may then provide the proper output based on this information.

However, with Deep Learning, your model can recognize photos of trucks and bicycles by sending data through numerous data processing layers in its framework. Structured data is not required. Deep Learning Frameworks rely on the output supplied at each data processing layer to generate accurate prediction. This data is then accumulated and presented as the final result. In this scenario, it eliminates all other options in order to stick with the sole legitimate answer.

We learn several essential truths from our examples above that will help you identify Deep Learning from Machine Learning as you learn over time. This may be summarized in the following ways:

Data Display

The major distinction between Machine Learning and Deep Learning may be seen in how we incorporate data into the two models. You will almost always need to utilize structured data when working with Machine Learning Models. Deep Learning networks, on the other hand, rely on artificial neural network layers to uncover unique characteristics that aid in data identification.

Algorithms and Human Intervention

The goal of Machine Learning is to learn by interacting with varied inputs and using patterns. Machine Learning Models may deliver better results as a result of such interaction the longer they learn and the more interaction they get. To help this cause, you should also aim to supply as much fresh data as feasible.

When you notice that the result supplied is not what you need, you must retrain the Machine Learning Model to produce a better output. As a result, even though the system is supposed to run without human interaction, you will need to be there from time to time.

Your presence is not required for Deep Learning. All of the hierarchical layers inside neural networks handle data at various levels. However, the model may make mistakes and learn from them along the process.

This is how the human brain works. As you get older, you acquire a lot of critical life skills via trial and error. By making errors, your brain learns the difference between good and negative feedback, and you strive for favorable outcomes whenever possible.

To be fair, your input will still be essential even in Deep Learning. You cannot be certain that the product will always be flawless. This is especially true when your input data is inadequate for the kind of output you want from the model.

The fundamental reason is that both Machine Learning and Deep Learning need data. The quality of your data will have a long-term influence on the output of these models. When it comes to data, you cannot just utilize whatever data you come across. To properly utilize any of these models, you must first understand how to evaluate data and ensure that you are using the right format for the model you want.

Labeled, structured data will often be required by Machine Learning Algorithms. As a result, they are not the greatest choice for solving complex issues that need large amounts of data.

In the case of distinguishing trucks from bicycles, we attempted to tackle a relatively easy problem in a theoretical idea. Deep Learning models, on the other hand, are used in more complicated models in the actual world. When you consider the procedures required, from ideas to hierarchical data processing and the various number of layers that data must travel through,

49

utilizing Deep Learning models to tackle basic issues is a waste of resources.

While all of these types of AI need data to help them conduct the intelligence we demand, Deep Learning models require substantially more data than Machine Learning Algorithms. This is significant because Deep Learning Algorithms must demonstrate beyond a reasonable doubt that their output is flawless before they can be approved.

PROGRAMMING ALGORITHMS

In programming, variables are the data storage, while algorithms are the building blocks. The data you need is retrieved by the program you use using algorithms. Algorithms serve as a link between natural language and computer language. Your problems are translated into the proprietary language used by your program before being translated back into a language you can understand and comprehend.

A culinary recipe is the simplest way to comprehend an algorithm. Recipes include every step of the process, from food preparation to the point at which the dish is ready to serve. This is what algorithms are capable of. They define the methods that your computer must follow to get your desired results.

While we're on the subject of recipes, we'd refer to them as processes in programming, ingredients as inputs, and the end result of your recipe as an output. Algorithms define how to carry out a job, and your computer will carry it out, in the same way, each time it is run.

To avoid misunderstanding, we must state that algorithms are not computer code. Algorithms are written in simple language that everybody can comprehend. It may be in English, Korean, or Chinese.

Algorithms are exact and are divided into three sections: the beginning, the middle, and the end. When creating an algorithm, you will provide the start and finish points for the first and final procedures.

Algorithms must only provide the information required to execute a job. They must be accurate in order to bring you to an effective answer. It is a good idea to number your processes while developing algorithms, however it is not required. Some programmers utilize pseudo-code, a semi-programming language that describes the steps in an algorithm.

Here's an example of a user email address request algorithm:
- Procedure 1: Start
- Procedure 2: Create variable to receive user email address
- Procedure 3: Clear variable if not empty
- Procedure 4: Request user email address
- Procedure 5: Store response in variable
- Procedure 6: Verify if email address is valid
- Procedure 7: Invalid address? Back to Procedure 3
- Procedure 8: End

Here's an example of a two-number addition algorithm:

Procedure 1: Start
Procedure 2: Declare variables num3, num4 also sum.
Procedure 3: Read variables num3 and num4.
Procedure 4: Add num3 to num4 and assign result to sum. um←num3+num4
Procedure 5: Display sum
Procedure 6: End

Here is an algorithm that determines the largest of three values:

Procedure 1: Start
Procedure 2: Declare the variables x, y and z.
Procedure 3: Read variables x, y and z.
Procedure 4: If x>y If x>z

Display x is largest number.
Else
Display z is largest number.

Else
If y>z
Display y is the largest number.
Else
Display z is largest number

Procedure 5: End

This is how simple algorithms are. They specify what you need in the operation. A good algorithm should contain the following characteristics:

- The input and output are defined clearly and precisely.
- All procedures must be basic and straightforward.
- The algorithm used should be the most efficient technique to arrive at a solution.
- An algorithm should not include any computer code.

In programming, you must learn about different types of algorithms and data structures. In developmental and competitive programming, you'll see them practically everywhere. The following are the key algorithms:

Algorithms for Sorting

This is one of the most extensive groups of algorithms that you may encounter in programming. These algorithms enable you to organize a list in the order that you choose. Today, each programming language has its sorting library. However, it is still necessary to be aware of the following:

- Sort by merging
- Sorting by count
- Sorting heaps

- Sorting by bucket
- Sort quickly
-

Understanding these algorithms isn't enough. What is more crucial is understanding how, where, and when they are required.

Algorithms for Search

There are two kinds of search algorithms: breadth-first search, which is used in group data structures, and binary search, which is used in linear data structures. When you require an efficient search on a sorted dataset, binary searches are advised. The idea here is to keep halving the dataset until you've narrowed your possibilities down to a single item. This technique is often used while searching for the name of a movie in a long list of movies. To get the correct answer, the program does a binary search using string matching.

When you need to locate the quickest feasible path from one location to another on your map, the search algorithm comes in helpful, particularly if you have a lot of alternatives. It is also used in AI to construct intelligent bots. Search engines are among the most frequent consumers of search algorithms since they comb the internet for relevant results before displaying them.

String Parsing and Matching

Pattern searching and matching will be one of the most difficult challenges you will face as a software writer. To do so, you must be familiar with the following:

- String comparison (KMP algorithm)

When it comes to matching small patterns in large strings, the Knuth-Morris-Pratt (KMP) method comes in handy. One such example is using the Ctrl+F command to search for a term.

Essentially, you are pattern matching the term pattern across the content.

- Parsing of strings (Regular expression)

You will also learn how to parse over established limits in order to verify texts in development, particularly when parsing and matching URLs in web development.

Algorithms for Hashing

Hash algorithms are among the most often used algorithms today, particularly when searching for a certain ID or key with relation to a dataset. The unique index of data obtained by hashing methods is used to identify it. Before the availability of hashing methods, similar searches were carried out using a mix of binary and sorting search techniques.

Hashing techniques allow you to search a list of objects to see whether a given value is already there. This method is also used by routers to recognize and store the IP addresses of devices connected to them. As a result, no two devices on the network may be allocated the same IP address.

Dynamic Programming

Dynamic programming techniques aid in problem-solving by breaking down complicated issues into smaller, more discernible pieces.

After then, each little unit is solved independently of the others, and the results are saved in memory. Once you've solved all of the little units, the answers will help you work your way up to the final solution to the complicated issue that prompted the algorithm.

Consider this: when you write 2+2+2+2+2, you know the answer is 10. If you add another +2 at the end, you get the answer 12 right away. You get to 12 so quickly because you already have the solution to the first set in your memory, so you only need to add one set of two. This is the operation of a dynamic programming algorithm.

Algorithms for Primality Testing

Probabilities and deterministic approaches may be used to determine if a random number is a prime number or not.
This method is widely used in cryptography, particularly in encryption and decryption. They are also employed as hash functions in hash tables.

Squaring Exponentiation

Try figuring out 232. You must do 32 computations involving the number 2 by default. This is an excessive amount of effort. This algorithm, on the other hand, just requires you to perform this 5 times. This method is also known as binary exponentiation.

Large positive integer powers in the format O can be computed relatively quickly using binary exponentiation (log2N). The example we've supplied is one of the most basic. Binary exponentiation is also useful for calculating square matrices and polynomial powers.

Managing Inheritance

The inheritances will be the subject of our next discussion here. These are a little more complicated than some of the other things in this manual, but at this time, you're ready to take on the challenge and truly work with something more difficult. When these inheritances are exposed, we will see some of the beauty that exists in the OOP languages that we discussed before, and we will be able to walk through and reuse sections of the code that we want to work with.

The inheritance idea is one of the most significant of all the concepts that come with OOP languages.

This concept will make it easy for us to create a class in our code depending on the terms of another class.

This is helpful since it makes it simpler to construct and manage one of the apps with which we wish to work.

It will also be important in allowing us to reuse the functionality of the code and complete the implementation quicker than ever before.

Instead of having to go through and write out brand new members of data and members of functions each time we want to build a class, the programmer may specify that the new class is expected to inherit the members of a class that is already present in the code.

This may be far more convenient than having to redefine the members and functions as you walk through the code time and again.

The base class will be the class on which we are basing our work or the current class.

The derived class is a new class that we are aiming to create, and it is the one that will use the base class's information, data, or functionalities.

The inheritance idea will be shown by using the "is a" connection.

It may, for example, function on the assumption that a mammal is an animal; the dog is a mammal, hence the dog is also an animal.

This will simplify the strategy we're using while still providing us with a clear picture of what we're up against along the way.

OUR INHERITANCE'S ACCESS CONTROL

The next topic to consider is access control and inheritance.

A derived class has access to all sections of the base class that are not already private.

This implies that when we do this, the members of the base class that should not be available to all of the member functions of the derived classes will be designated as private for the base class.

As we go through this, you'll note that the derived class will be able to inherit all of the base class's methods.

There will be a few alternative exceptions that we may utilize with this one depending on the effects we want to achieve. Among the exceptions to this rule that we must keep in mind are:

1. The friend functions that are found with our base class.

2. The overloaded operators that come with our base class.

3. Any destructors, constructors, or copy constructors that will occur with our base class.

We must pay close attention to some of the many components that appear with our access control.

If certain constraints are discovered in our base class, this will create some complications with the inheritance that we are dealing with.

And the kid or derived class will be aware of this along the way.

Inheritance Types

While we're here, let's take a closer look at the sorts of inheritances we can deal with.

When we attempt to derive a class from one of our base classes in the first place, the base class may be inherited through a private, protected, or public inheritance.

The access specifier, which we discussed before, will be used to specify the kind of inheritance that you utilize.

Now, you will see that it is uncommon for us to deal with a private or protected inheritance, while it is feasible.

Just be aware that there may be some challenges along the road that will be difficult to deal with.

Public inheritance is the technique that we are most likely to use here. Even though the public option will be the most usual for us to deal with, we must consider some of the rules that will apply when we work with the various forms of inheritance.

The several guidelines that we must remember while dealing with this one are as follows:

The Inheritance of the People

When we wish to derive a new class from a public base class, the public members of the base, or original class, become public members of the derived class.

The protected members contained in our base class will subsequently become protected members of some of the derived classes that we create from it.

a. As one may expect, we will discover that the private members located in our base class are never immediately available from the derived class.
b. We can go to them from here.

c. To make this happen, we just need to make some calls to the protected and public elements of our base class.

The Safeguarded Inheritance

The second option is protected inheritance, which we can deal with.

When we wish to derive a new class from a protected base class, the protected and public members of the base class will become protected members of the derived class that we want to work with.

Personal Inheritance

The third sort of inheritance we will look at is private inheritance. When we attempt to derive a new class from a private base class, both the protected and public members of our base class will be transferred to the derived class, but they will be converted into some of the private members instead.

As we can see, each of them will be distinct from the others.

And it is for this reason that we must be cautious about the kind of inheritances with which we will be working. If you have a different form of inheritance, the members will not always operate the way you want them to.

61

Check what you're in and make sure it's set to the appropriate sort so that it operates the way you want it to.

SYNTAX

A computer programming language's syntax is also known as its grammar and spelling. The computer has its own language, and it can only execute an operation if it is entered in the language that the computer knows. This language is known as Syntax. A system of rules that explains the combinations of computer symbols that are part of any element in a computer language or recognized to be a correctly organized document is also characterized as a syntax of computer programming. Syntax programming often comprises strings that are similar to words; when these strings are correctly synthesized, they form accurate and legitimate sentences. The communication flow may alter due to program differences, but syntax remains the communication flow between programmers and their machines. It specifies how a program should be written and interpreted, and Syntax errors are unavoidable if the language of the program is not properly understood by the programmer.

Syntax and Its Importance in Computer Programming

Syntax is simply the use of organized language that the computer can comprehend, and when a user fails to use a language that the computer can understand, mistakes may occur and the programming instruction will fail to execute. The Syntax is also known as a bridge or a medium of communication between you and your computer. The goal of Syntax is to be able to operate on a computer efficiently and without mistake.

Furthermore, the quality of Syntax simplifies and simplifies a work.

It also facilitates reading and comprehending code.

What exactly is a syntax error?

A Syntax Error may occur when the sequence of characters are not written correctly, or the compiler or interpreter cannot understand the source code, so as to generate a machine code. It may also occur if an erroneous equation is included.

Syntax Levels

Syntax of Words

All of the essential symbols of the computer language in use are included in Lexical Syntax. A Lexeme is a series of characters in a computer. A Lexical Syntax, on the other hand, is a logical language composed of grammatical rules that define a collection of Lexemes.

Syntax of Concrete

Concrete syntax is a collection of principles that govern how expressions, programs, and statements are written and understood. It specifies how language components have been shown and altered. The Concrete Syntax represents the program's appearance to the programmer.

Syntax of Abstraction

The internal representation of certain programs by the simplicity of their grammar is defined as abstract syntax. Abstract Syntax refers to the implementation of a language. The Abstract Syntax explains how a program appears to an evaluator or compiler.

Syntax Programming Varieties

There are several Syntax Programming Languages, each of which is different from the others.

Prolog Syntax and Semantics are a collection of principles that govern how to write and understand a prolog program. Because Prolog is logic and declarative language, the programmer must think differently about the programs. Prolog Syntax was one of the earliest languages developed, and it is still widely used in other languages today. It is beneficial for theorem proving, expert systems, term rewriting, automated planning, and natural language planning.

Perl Syntax draws syntax from various languages such as Bourbe Shell, Lisp, and Smalltalk. The Perl Syntax is a versatile programming language that may be modified or changed in any way the programmer desires. The Perl Syntax has both declaration and statement sequences, and every statement in Perl must finish with a semicolon. It is also a case-sensitive programming language that does not permit characters and punctuation such as @, $, and percent.

PHP Syntax and Semantics are a collection of principles that govern how to write and understand PHP programs. The PHP Syntax was designed to be compatible with the C Syntax format, allowing it to be utilized in web development.

C syntax is essentially a collection of principles that a programmer must follow while developing a C program. The C program is made up of pieces such as header files, the main function, and program code. Because C syntax is case sensitive, a programmer must follow the rules for the C program to avoid Syntax Error.

Every C statement must be followed by a semicolon, and every C command must be typed in lower case characters. The C language is represented by numbers in three different forms: integral, real, and complex.

C++ Syntax is a programming language that was created as an extension to the C programming language by a Danish computer scientist named Bjarne Stroustrup. C++ Syntax is utilized in a wide range of application sectors, making it a general-purpose language and an International Organization for Standardization standard.
Although C++ inherits much of C's syntax characteristics, it provides more efficient hardware access and abstractions than other languages.

Java syntax is a collection of rules that explains how to write and understand a Java program. Java, on the other hand, was developed from both C and C++ syntax. Despite these derivations, there are a few distinctions between both languages: there are no accessible variables or global functions in Java, but there are data members that are considered global variables.

JavaScript syntax is the collection of rules that a programmer must follow before creating or reading a JavaScript program. JavaScript distinguishes between two sorts of values: fixed values known as literals and changeable values known as variables. JavaScript literals are important rules that define how fixed values should be written, and the values are guided by the following rules:

- Numbers may be written with or without decimal points.

- Strings are text or words that are typed between a single and double quotation.

JavaScript variables are used to hold data values, however, the var keyword is used to define variables. The var keyword merely denotes a variable, which may be altered at any moment.

Some of Java's characteristics are derived from Java Syntax, while others are inherited from Awk and Perl. Despite some resemblance to Java Syntax, it is a completely separate language from JavaScript Syntax. JavaScript is case-sensitive, and a programmer must keep this in mind while creating a statement.

Python syntax and semantics are a collection of principles that regulate how Python programs are written and understood. The Python program was designed with readability in mind, and it uses English terms more often, if not exclusively than other languages.

Furthermore, the Python language has some parallels to Perl, C, and Java syntax, as well as some fundamental variances. A Python program, on the other hand, is split into logical lines that are made up of one or two physical lines. When this logical line is ended, the to-ken newline is normally used.

In computer programming, a line consists of just tabs, spaces, and occasionally a remark is known as a black line, which is normally disregarded by the Python interpreter. A physical line, on the other hand, is a group of character sequences that conclude at the end-of-life sequence. The following terms are reserved in Python syntax: false, class, finally, none, continue, for, from, global, as, assert, break, and so on.

Lua Syntax is a high-level multi-paradigm that comprises a large number of instructions designed for a particular application and job execution. The Lua programming language enables programmers to create namespaces, classes, and other features. Lua is a basic and versatile language; Haskell Syntax is a multidimensional language, and here are a few reasons why. Haskell Syntax is a language that may be used to write any kind of program, which is why it is referred to as a general-purpose language.

67

It is also a statically typed language, which allows it to fit into any application. Haskell programs are separated into two phases: compile time and run time. It is a compiled time phase where each of your variables has a type that determines the sort of data the variable is authorized to retain. Statically typed languages include Java and C Syntax.

Furthermore, Haskell allows you to write anonymous functions, store them in variables, and give them as arguments to other functions. The Haskell language functions always yield the same result and value.

The syntax of SQL

I feel you have a good understanding of what Syntax is all about by now. The syntax is just adhering to the syntax and rules that govern computer languages. SQL, like every other language, has its unique syntax. When used in SQL, every punctuation mark, symbol, and letter has significance. Every SQL command must terminate with a semicolon. When developing a command, whether in SQL or another programming language, it is essential that you study and follow the rules. If the punctuation or letters are utilized incorrectly, leaving too much space or using a capital letter might result in a Syntax Error.

It is easy to avoid syntax errors if you constantly write a clear and succinct programming command.

Making Your Very First Database

Before you can have a successful database with useful tables in SQL programming, you must first create a database and then a table. There is, however, a variety of SQL data application applications available, all of which have a nearly identical procedure of establishing a new database and tables. When you develop your first database system, you must design a table into which you will feed your data and store it more securely and efficiently. SQL provides a free graphical user interface that is simple to design. Before you think about feeding your data, here's a step-by-step instruction on how to establish your first SQL database and tables.

Steps

Step 1: Install the SQL Server Management Studio software.

The first step in building your first database and table is to download the SQL software from Microsoft, which is accessible for free online.

This program is pre-installed and allows you to interface with and control the SQL server using just a few command-line commands.

Furthermore, it is critical when accessing databases in distant areas. Mac users, on the other hand, may navigate the Database system using open-source tools such as SQuirrel SQL.

Step 2: Open SQL Studio.

When you run SQL Studio, the program may periodically ask for a server that you will want to use all along or the one you are now using. If you already have one, you may select to enter the permissions, authenticate, and connect. Some people choose to use local database systems by creating a new name and authenticating using a desired name or address. The procedure of engaging with the program and establishing your first database and table starts with the launch of the SQL server management studio.

Step 3: Locate the Database Folder

A window will appear on the left of the screen immediately after connecting on either the local or remote. On top of that, there will be a server to which it will connect. If not, click on the '+' symbol, which will reveal many items, including the option to create a new database. In certain versions, the icon for establishing a new database may appear instantly on the left drop-down window.

After that, click 'Create New Database.'

Step 4: Construct a New Database

As noted in step 3, the drop-down menu will reveal all available choices, including the option to create a new database. First, you will configure the database based on your specifications and provide a name for easy identification. Most users prefer to leave the settings alone, but you may modify them if you understand how they affect your data storage process in the system. It is important to note that when you establish the database name, two files will be generated automatically: data and log files. Data files are in charge of storing data, while log files keep account of any updates, additions, and other adjustments made to the database.

Step 5: Design Your Tables

Databases often do not hold data unless structures in the form of rows and tables are constructed to keep that data structured. Tables are the main storage units for data, but you must first build the table before inserting the data. Tables, like building a new database, are simple to create. Expand the window in the Databases folder, then right-click on Tables and choose 'Nee Table.'

Windows will launch, presenting a table that may be readily customized in terms of the number of rows and columns, titles, and how you wish to arrange your work. In this stage, you will be successful in establishing both the database and the table, allowing you to go further in arranging your assignment.

Step 6: Create the Primary Key

The primary key is important in databases because it serves as a record number or ID for simple identification and recollection when viewing the page later. As a result, it is strongly advised that these keys be created in the first column. There are other methods to do this, including inserting the ID in the column field by typing 'int' and deselecting the 'Allow Nulls' checkbox. Choose the key icon from the toolbar and set it as the primary key.

Step 7: Arrange the Tables

Tables often include numerous columns, also known as fields, and each column represents a different aspect of data inputs. When you first created your table, you designed it to suit the number of data entries, which is why additional primary keys are required for each dataset. As a result, the structuring process will require associating each column with a specific collection of data. For example, there are columns for the first name, last name, and address, among others.

Step 8: Adding More Columns

You will see that new columns appear underneath the columns for main keys as soon as you create them. These are not for main keys but are required for the entry of additional information. As a result, be careful to enter the right data for each column to prevent populating the table with incorrect information. In the column, you will input the data types 'nchar' for text, 'int' for whole numbers, and 'decimal' for decimal values.

Step 9: Make a copy of the table.

When you've finished filling out the material in each field, you'll see that your table has rows and columns. However, before inputting the data, you must first save the table. This may be accomplished by choosing the Save icon in the toolbar and naming your table. When naming your table, be sure to choose a name that is readily related to or recognized by the content. Furthermore, databases with various tables should have distinct names so that they can be readily recognized.

Step 10: Enter Data

After saving the table, you may enter the data into the system, populating each column with appropriate information. However, you can check to see whether the table has been saved by opening the Tables Folder and looking for our table name. If you don't see your table, utilize the Table Folder to refresh the tables and you'll see it. Back in the table, right-click on the table to bring up a drop dialog box, and then pick 'Edit Top 200 Rows.' The Window will then show fields for you to enter data into, but disregard the main keys since they will be filled automatically. Continue in this manner until you have entered the final data into the table.

Step 11: Putting the Table Together

You must save the material when you have completed working on the table so that you do not lose your work. Because the table has already been saved, after you complete inputting data, click 'Execute SQL' on the toolbar, and the procedure of feeding each data you entered into the columns will be executed. Depending on the amount of data, the processing process may take a few seconds. If there are any faults in the feeding process, the system will display the areas where you entered data improperly.

Furthermore, you may run the program that parses all of the data by pressing 'ctrl' and 'R.'

Step 12: Querying the Data

At this point, you've built your first database and table, and you've successfully stored the data using SQL language programming. The database is now fully operational, and you may now create additional tables inside a single database. However, there is a limit to the number of tables that may be stored in a database, although many users seem unconcerned about this restriction. As a result, you may establish new database systems and tables as needed. You may then query your data for reports or any other relevant reasons, such as organizational or administrative ones. Having a broad understanding of SQL programming, particularly when it comes to establishing databases and tables, often assists you to increase your learning abilities.

USING THE COMMAND-LINE TO CREATE YOUR FIRST DATABASE AND TABLE

SQL commands and statements are used to build databases and tables. The same is true for SQL Server Management Studio as it is for the previous tutorial, however commands and statements are used to tell the system to do a certain function. To construct your first database, run the command 'SELECT DATABASE (database name)' and then press the execute button. As a result, the notification on the screen should read 'Command(s) finished successfully,' indicating that your database has been established.

To utilize the database, type 'USE (database name),' which instructs the query window to launch the new database application. Creating a new table, on the other hand, necessitates using the command 'CREATE TABLE (table name).' Entering data is as simple as typing 'INSERT DATA INTO (table name), VALUES (table name),' and then repeating the procedure for each dataset you have. The same lets you inspect the stored data and provides the command format 'SELECT * FROM (table name).' When it comes to navigating multiple SQL databases, all of the instructions listed above are crucial. As a result, it is always necessary to master each SQL fundamental instruction in order to run programs quickly.

Working with Well-Known Apps

Machines have many applications that operate alone or in conjunction with other programs without causing harm to other programs in the system until activated. When you launch one app, for example, it tends to execute its basic duties with little interference from other apps that are currently running. Following that, this phase will go through common programs used as programming language tools, particularly in database management systems. It is important to remember that computer programs are created by a variety of developers, with some developing more than one, such as major corporations like Microsoft.

As a result, the functioning and design of distinct computer applications vary greatly.

SQLite is being used.

SQLite, unlike other database management systems, is a relational database management system (RDBMS) rather than a client-server database. Richard Hipp created the software, which was originally published in August 2000. SQLite is vital as an embedded database program and as a storage application for both client and local storage on systems such as web browsers. As a result, it is commonly utilized in database engines since it easily binds to many programming languages. As a result, it is critical for operating systems, embedded devices, and web browsers.

SQLite operates differently from other databases such as MySQL, Oracle, and SQL Servers since its objective is to tackle a distinct challenge when it comes to local data storage for individual usage. SQLite is suited for the internet of things and embedded devices such as smartphones in this scenario since it lacks an administrative role and thrives at network edges. SQLite, as previously said, is also necessary for websites for medium and low traffic database use. It is also useful for on-disk file formatting and data analysis for larger datasets using the SQLite3 command-line shell. Other uses include business data caching, information transmission, file archiving, ad hoc replacement, and use as a teaching tool for educational reasons.

Apache OpenOffice Base is being used.

Apache OpenOffice is a database system that is a fork of OpenOffice.org that includes a word processor, spreadsheet, presentation software, drawing program, database management software, and formula editor. Apache OpenOffice can write a variety of file formats, including Microsoft Office, and is available for Linux, Windows, and macOS. It is an Apache Software Foundation product that was first launched in May 2018. Furthermore, it is an open office productivity program that is simple to use since it combines all other file types, can be used immediately after purchase and is supported by thousands of users.

PostgreSQL is being used.

PostgreSQL, often known as Postgre, is another free and opensource RDBMS built to manage large workloads from individual computers for commercial usage. It focuses on extensibility and technological standards that are designed particularly for Mac users. Versions of Linux, Windows, and other operating systems are, nonetheless, available. PostgreSQL, created by the PostgreSQL Global Development Group, was originally released to the market in July 1996. As a database management system, this program enables transaction isolation as well as atomicity and consistency in data processing. The latest improvements enable for user-friendly interfaces suited for the insertion of custom functions required for programming languages such as Python, JavaScript, and C/C+. Development started in 1982.

Using Adobe ColdFusion

ColdFusion, which was first launched in 1995, is commercial software mostly used for online application development. It was designed by J. J. Allaire and improved by Adobe Systems Incorporated as a programming language to connect HTML sites to databases, and it featured an IDE in 1996. Using Adobe ColdFusion enables you to explore a new system full of unique capabilities for dealing with various sorts of data. It comes with an expressive and powerful function that makes the building and design of current web application software easier when compared to other programming languages. Adobe ColdFusion, as a database management system, enables users to access simplified databases while also providing additional advantages such as client/server administration, code creation, and operational graphics, among others.

PHP Programming

PHP (Hypertext Preprocessor) is a versatile scripting computer language created in 1994 by Rasmus Lerdorf and published in 1995. It was originally known as Personal Home Pages, and it was used to create static and dynamic web pages, as well as online apps.

PHP-generated scripts can only be read and understood by servers that have a PHP application installed. Using PHP is one method for learning how to code values, which leads to the creation of newer versions of web applications. PHP was used on web servers, command lines, client-side graphical user interfaces, and was supported by a variety of web hosting systems. When dealing with PHP, it allows users to easily operate, construct, modify, and have their extension.

Using the IBM Db2 database

Db2 is a collection of database products, including servers, created by IBM that was initially launched in 1993. It is compatible with Linux, Windows, and UNIX operating systems written in C/C+, Java, and assembly. It supports a variety of functionalities, including object-relational and non-relational features like XML.

In comparison to SQL, Db2 similarly accompanies tables but also adds objects, such as indexes important data containers, such as table's spades. While SQL is a common computer programming language that focuses on data tables retrieved in a relational database, the Db2 family includes databases, warehouses, BigSQL, event stores, and cloud-oriented objects such as warehouses on the cloud. As it fits with focused aspects critical for system functioning, the usage of IBM Db2 enables for data storage, analysis, and fast retrieval when needed.

Making Use of Oracle Express

Oracle Express is a web-based program that operates on Oracle database servers. It was initially released in 2004 by Oracle Corporation. It supports a variety of operating systems, including Linux, Oracle Scolaris, and HP-UX, which are required for the development of sophisticated web applications used in current web browsers. Oracle Express supports system menu commands and database home pages, which aid in the creation of settings that assist its tasks. System menu commands enable users to access the database's original functionality, while home pages are essential for completing many database management duties.

Monitoring database storage and sessions, as well as startup settings, are among the features. The usage of Oracle Express enables a user to execute values that aid in computer languages that are essential for current web browsers.

Making Use of MariaDB

MariaDB is a MySQL relational database management system that is also available as a free and open-source program. MariaDB, which was released in October 2009, was meant to be extremely compatible with the MySQL database. However, over time, the compatibility has grown to become a drop-in alternative for the usage of MySQL. When compared to MySQL, MariaDB is much quicker and more secure, with current upgrades occurring up to twice as often. Furthermore, you may combine data from MariaDB with other database systems while only utilizing one node at a time. MariaDB can connect to many databases again, although the method varies based on the operating system.

Making Use of Microsoft

Access Microsoft Access was initially launched in November 1992, after it had been created, designed, and improved by Microsoft. The application has gained popularity and is generally used for personal use due to its ability to connect and retrieve data saved in other applications and databases. It has also aided software developers and engineers, data architects, and power users in the development of additional applications. Microsoft Access is still supported by Visual Basic for Applications and ActiveX Data Objects, allowing it to be utilized in reports.

Making Use of Microsoft

Microsoft has also included Microsoft SQL Server, which is another relational database management system utilized as a software product for data storage and retrieval when software programs request it. Different audiences, including other concurrent users, utilize the software on both small-scale and large-scale internet-facing projects. Microsoft SQL Server was initially introduced in April 1989 and is now available in a variety of versions to meet a variety of purposes, including online, enterprise, express, and business intelligence.

There are additional special versions such as azure, fast track, compact (SQL CE), and analytics platform systems, as well as discontinued editions such as MSDE, personal edition, and datacenter. As a user, Microsoft SQL Servers are critical for the systematic structuring of data, allowing for efficient data retrieval.

Making Use of Microsoft ASP

Microsoft ASP (Active Server Pages) is a computer language developed by Microsoft that is used for dynamic web pages. It was popular in the 1990s. It was used in Windows 95 and 98, and it was a scripting computer programming language that allowed for easy code that was integrated with HTML and ran on servers. The ASP file extension is. asp and the program is typically transmitted to the browser, however, this may be altered. Furthermore, Microsoft ASP supports the use of additional computer languages in the script, including Jscript. Despite being an older database management system, ASP allows for ease of use by allowing lines of code to be instantly placed in an online form with a URL. As a consequence, APS becomes more participatory, and results are obtained without the need for extensive programming abilities. Microsoft ASP, unlike other database programming packages, enables the addition of functionality. As a consequence, it has produced more effective outcomes, and it is still in use today among contemporary variants.

ASP.NET (Microsoft)

ASP.NET is a current Microsoft ASP format that comes with an open-source and web application server that is required for web development in order to create dynamic web pages. The application was launched in January 2002, enabling programmers to take use of contemporary ASP capabilities to create dynamic webpages, programs, and apps. Unlike ASP, ASP.NET supports a wider range of programming models, including ASP.NET web forms, MVC, web API, signalR, and web pages. The tools used in ASP.NET were developed by Microsoft and other firms with the purpose of fine-tuning productive outputs. The application is available for free download to all users, and it is then installed and activated to allow you to easily run applications.

Making Use of Microsoft Query

Microsoft database management software is a query that allows users to acquire visual methods for database querying by using text string examples, file names, and document lists, as it includes query by example tools. The application works by allowing the system to convert inputs into formal database queries using SQL. As a result, users may easily conduct sophisticated searches as a type of data retrieval without requiring SQL knowledge or expertise. Microsoft Query makes advantage of the Query-by-Example capability, which was developed by NY Moshe M. Zloof in the 1970s.

Furthermore, it employs the Microsoft Access user-friendly interface, enabling learners to quickly learn and comprehend relational database management systems for usage in small enterprises. The Microsoft Query program is also used as an embedded tool in a spreadsheet in Access.

HANDLING EXCEPTIONS

What Is a Bug?

Bugs have to be the most despised monsters that a programmer may have. A bug in the eyes of a coder is a bug in a program. These flaws have the potential to create mistakes or undesired effects. A problem may often be corrected after the fact. Of sure, there are irreversible lessons. Within a minute after its initial flight, the European Ariane 5 rocket detonated. An after-action analysis found that the navigator was supposed to convert a floating-point number to an integer, but the amount was too big to overflow. In addition, in 1994, a British helicopter crashed, killing 29 people. According to the study, the helicopter's software system was "full of problems." In the 2001 film "A Space Odyssey," the supercomputer HAL murders virtually all of the astronauts due to a conflict between two aims in its program.

In English, a bug is a flaw. For many years, engineers have used the word bug to refer to mechanical flaws. There's also a tale regarding how the term "bug" was used in software development. A moth once flew into an early computer, causing it to malfunction. Since then, the term "bug" has been used to refer to bugs. The moth was eventually published in a journal and is now on exhibit at the National Museum of American History.

Code:

```
for result in range(5)  print(result) Output is:
```

SyntaxError: invalid Syntax

There are no syntax issues in the following program, yet when Python is executed, the reference's subscript is beyond the scope of the list element.

result= [12, 24, 36]

The program aborts the error reporting Output:

The above-mentioned form of Error, which the compiler discovers only at runtime, is referred to as a Runtime Error. Because Python is a dynamic language, many actions, such as identifying the type of a variable, must be done at run time. As a consequence, unlike a static language, Python is more prone to run-time mistakes.

A Semantic Error is a different form of Error. The compiler believes that your software is correct and that it can execute properly. However, with closer inspection of the software, it becomes clear that it is not what you want to accomplish. In general, such mistakes are the most pervasive and toughest to remedy. Here's an example of a program that prints the first entry of a list.

mix = ["first", "second", "third"]

print(mix[1])

Normal print, no errors in the software. However, you discover that you print out the second element, B, rather than the first element.

This is because the Python list begins with a subscript beginning with 0, therefore to refer to the first member, the subscript should be 0, not 1.

Debugging

Debugging is the process of repairing a problem in a program. Because computer programs are deterministic, there is always an opportunity for mistakes. Of course, spending a significant amount of time unable to debug a program might result in a strong sense of dissatisfaction, or even the belief that you are unsuitable for program development. Others pound the keyboard, believing the machine is amusing itself. Even the finest programmers, in my opinion, will have defects while writing programs. It's simply those competent programmers are more at ease with debugging and don't second-guess themselves when it comes to errors.

Debugging is similar to being a detective. Gather the evidence, remove the suspects, and leave the true murderer alone.

There are several methods and techniques for gathering evidence. To begin, you don't need to devote much effort to these tools. You can view the condition of the variable and how far it has run by putting a simple print() function within the program. You may sometimes test your idea by substituting one instruction with another and seeing how the program output changes. When all other alternatives are ruled out, the genuine reason for the mistake remains.

Debugging, on the other hand, is a natural aspect of developing programs. Test-Driven Development is one method for creating a software (TDD).Python is such an easy-to-use, dynamic language that it's a smart place to start is by developing a simple program that does a certain purpose. Then, on the basis of the little program, progressively adjust the program so that it continues to expand and, eventually, meets the difficult criteria. You keep adding features and repairing problems throughout the process. The crucial thing to remember is that you've been coding. Python's creator like this kind of programming. So, debugging is an essential technique if you want to develop the correct application.

Exceptional Detail Handling

We can deal with mistakes that may arise during runtime in advance of the application. This might have two objectives. The first is to enable the application to complete more activities before aborting, such as giving more information about the mistake. The second option is to keep the software running after it creates an error.

Exception handling may also help to increase the fault tolerance of software. Exception handling is used in the following procedure:

A try structure is used to enclose the software that needs exception handling. Except describes how the program should react when a certain mistake occurs. Input() is a built-in function that accepts command-line input. To convert other sorts of data to floating-point values, utilize the float() method. If you input a string, such as "P," it will not be transformed to a floating-point number, resulting in a ValueError, and the related except will execute the program associated with it. If you input 0, dividing by 0 will result in a ZeroDivisionError. Because the default program handles both problems, the program does not abort.

The complete Syntax for exception handling is:

try:

... (code should be written here)

except exception1:

... (code should be written here)

except exception2:

... (code should be written here)

else:

... (code should be written here)

finally:

If an exception occurs inside a try, the exception is allocated and the except function is called. Layer by layer, check to see whether it is exception1, exception2, and so on and then run the associated instructions in except. If there is no exception in a try, the except component bypasses the otherwise statement execution. Finally, whether or not there is an exception, is something you do at the end. If except is followed by no arguments, the application will handle all exceptions.

GATHERING YOUR DATA

The first thing we need to consider is how to collect the data required to complete this kind of activity in data science. We need to be able to sift through our data and find out what type of info is out there that we can exploit, among other things. However, determining where to get that data, how much to gather, and what kind would be most useful in helping us learn more about our consumers and business may be difficult.

When it comes to the kind of data that we want to utilize along the road, there are a plethora of alternatives available. We must ensure that we are gathering the correct kind of data, rather than just collecting data because it is available and seems to be the right thing to work with. It will be crucial if we can arrange information in the manner that we want and ensure that we truly get solid data, even if it is not initially organized and structured in the manner that we like.

That is why we will spend some time in this phase discussing what we can do with our data, how it will work for our purposes, and even some of the areas where you may search to get the data that you want to work with. With that in mind, let's get started!

Know what your biggest business issue is.

There is a lot of data out there, and it won't take long for you to get yourself in a rabbit hole with all of it if you don't have a strategy or a direction for what you're going to do with it. There is a lot of wonderful data out there, but if you let it lead you instead of having a clear road in front of you, you'll have a lot of issues and never receive the decision-making assistance you need.

If you've already collected your data, this step is complete, and we can go on to the next step. You may think about your main company issue, the one you'd want to spend your time focused on and address, and then filter through the data there to see what improvements you can make and what data from that vast source would make the most impact. Don't be afraid to save some of the data for later, and don't allow the fact that you won't be able to utilize part of it to deter you.

During this time, we want to focus on learning the most up-to-date information; this is the ideal method to ensure that you acquire the knowledge you need to move your company forward.

It's acceptable if part of the information is left behind. If you need part of it later, you may go back to it. However, for your algorithms to provide the greatest results, you should only utilize the best data you have.

Now, if you haven't had the opportunity to go out and gather data yet, that's something we can work with. Forming the issue you want to address and having a clear route will help you filter through all of the noise and guarantee that you can get things done. You need to make sure you're looking in the appropriate areas for the information that'll be most vital for what you're trying to do, the portion that'll be so crucial when it comes time to tackle some of the jobs that's out there.

Where Should You Look for Data?

The next step in this process of acquiring data and applying it in the way we want is determining where to discover and seek the information we want. There are a lot of various areas where we may go for the data we need, but that's part of the appeal of today's contemporary system.

However, we must keep in mind that the majority of the data we acquire today will not be categorized or structured. This isn't a major concern since we'll look at some of the actions you can take to arrange the data later. Just be aware that you will have to go through and do a few more procedures to ensure that your data is structured in the way that you like, and that it will not be as clean and tidy as you would like in the long term.

As a result, the areas where you may hunt for some of the data that you want to utilize in this process will vary, and it will frequently rely on what you want to get out of it. However, you should focus on obtaining the highest-quality data possible throughout the process. This will guarantee that you can locate the data you want and that the algorithms you use later on will be capable of providing you with some of the greatest results and insights you require to propel your company ahead.

There are still several locations where you may seek the information you need. You'll discover that you can get data from websites (particularly if you want to work with web scraping), social networking sites (if you're using one), your surveys and focus groups, and other firms that may have gathered the data and are utilizing it to aid others along the path.

You could discover that bringing up data from a more distinctive source can help you get even farther ahead with some of the tasks you wish to do. It will guarantee that you have data that no one else has and will present you with fresh patterns and insights, as long as you ensure that the data is of high quality and will be suitable for your purposes.

Where Should the Data Be Stored?

Along the way, we'll need to think about where we'd want to keep some of the data we're working with. You're going to collect a lot of data in the process, and you're not going to want to leave it lying about without a purpose or in a safe and secure area. This is particularly true if you're dealing with data that you've collected yourself, such as data from surveys or other sources that you don't want people to see.

There are a variety of locations where you might keep this data for your requirements, and the one you pick will frequently be determined by what works best for you. This might be a good place to start if you have adequate storage space on your network. The data is therefore always safe and secure with you and easily accessible. You only need to make sure that your system has some excellent security measures in place so that you don't lose that information and no longer have access to it.

Many businesses choose to store information in the cloud, which is a web-based storage place. This provides an additional layer of security for the data while also ensuring that you can access it when you need it. There are many different types of storage places with which we may work, and you will discover that you can make this work for some of your demands. Whether your storage requirements are vast or little, you will discover that keeping this data will make a significant impact when it comes time to manage this procedure, and all you have to do now is pick how much you want to utilize.

It'll be critical to know where to go for the data you'll need to get started on your data analysis and data science project. This will establish the tone for the work you'll be able to perform later on, as well as the level of success you'll have with your project. Make sure to look for the data you'll need and consider how much you'll need, where you'll likely find it, and other factors.

CONCLUSION

The handbook comes to an end here. The next step is to use your newfound knowledge of Basic Programming, Data Science, Data Analysis, and Machine Learning to good use, which has resulted in the formation of the powerhouse known as "Silicon Valley." When it comes to data analysis, a wide range of businesses in a variety of sectors may profit. This helps them to get a lot of the power and authority they want for their particular sectors, ensuring that they will be able to wow their clients and achieve positive outcomes in the process. Learning how to utilize a data analysis will alter the game in terms of how you conduct business, as long as you use it correctly.

We wish to congratulate you for making it through the first Procedures of this amazing trip as a novice programmer. Now that your feet have crossed the barrier, we welcome you to have a look around and let your imagination run wild. When you set your mind to anything, there is no limit to what you can achieve.

You've been taught the fundamentals of programming. You've had to deal with a slew of syntax errors, exceptions, and the possibility of a system crash. You've now been introduced to the world of programming. So, how do you go from here?

The solution is straightforward: follow the wind.

You should know what you want to accomplish with your newly learned programming abilities at this stage. You must make your path as the magician you are today, deciding how to best use your power. For example, the majority of the job of programmers entails the use of Application Program Interfaces (APIs) (APIs). As a result, the need for data collection and processing is never-ending.

When it comes to your well-being, nothing beats knowing what's out there for you to discover. Your programming skills are in demand in a wide range of fields.

These examples may assist you in deciding which path to choose.

Data scientists need programmers because Python is an excellent tool with numerous modules that address many of the limitations of other languages. The most essential factor, though, is how well programmers are compensated.

Machine learning is best practiced in programming, while it is supported by libraries in other computer languages.

None, however, come close to Python. Corporations such as Google, as well as thousands of programmers all around the globe, utilize it.

Web development using Python and Django makes creating web apps a breeze. If you're passionate about it, you can do in minutes what other developers would take hours to accomplish.

Whatever path you follow from here, know that you are prepared to tackle any problems you may encounter. We firmly think that you now possess some of the most useful informative bullets available, as well as sufficient tips and techniques to get you started in the world of codes. View this as an adventure, just like everything else in life, and don't be afraid to go out and explore new territory. There's still a lot more than programming has to offer, and if you're a programmer seeking more sophisticated methods and insights, simply check into it. You'll learn more the more you do, and you'll want to learn more.

I hope you've taken something away from this!

www.ingramcontent.com/pod-product-compliance
Lightning Source LLC
LaVergne TN
LVHW041338200726
843509LV00009B/766